QUICK COOKING

TARLA DALAL
India's # 1 Cookery Author

S&C
SANJAY & CO.
MUMBAI

Second Printing : 2006

Copyright © Sanjay & Co.

ISBN : 81-89491-12-1

All rights reserved with the publishers.

No part of this book may be reproduced, stored in a retrieval system or transmitted by any means, electronic, mechanical, photocopying, recording or otherwise, without the written permission of the publishers.

Price: Rs.89/-

Published & Distributed by : **Sanjay & Company**

353/A-1, Shah & Nahar Industrial Estate, Dhanraj Mill Compound,

Lower Parel (W), Mumbai - 400 013. INDIA.

Tel. : (91-22) 2496 8068 • Fax : (91-22) 2496 5876 • E-mail : sanjay@tarladalal.com

Printed by : **Minal Sales Agencies**, Mumbai

Recipe Research & Production Design Arati Fedane Sana Paloba	**Copy Editor** Nisha Katira **Food Styling** Shubhangi Dhaimade	**Photography** Jignesh Jhaveri **Typesetting** Adityas Enterprises	**Design** Satyamangal Rege

DISCLAIMER

While every precaution has been taken in the preparation of this book, the publishers and the author assume no responsibility for errors or omissions. Neither is any liability assumed for damages resulting from the use of information contained herein. And of course, no book is a substitute for a qualified medical advice. So it is wiser to modify your dietary patterns under the supervision of a doctor or a nutritionist.

BULK PURCHASES

Tarla Dalal Cookbooks are ideal gifts. If you are interested in buying more than 500 assorted copies of Tarla Dalal Cookbooks at special prices, please contact us at 91-22-2496 8068 or email : sanjay@tarladalal.com

INTRODUCTION

Dear Friends,

In today's fast-paced and stressed out lives, where leisure time or 'a time to relax' is a phenomena of the past, working individuals find themselves in some sort of a frenzy when it comes to regular day-to-day cooking. After a hard day's work, no one feels like toiling in the kitchen chopping onions and inhaling the fumes of the masalas. Keeping in mind this scenario, I have come up with this excellent book, which is a compilation of several, easy to cook, nutritious recipes made in a matter of minutes be it a hot Creamy Vegetable Soup on a cool winter's night or a chilled Herbal Macaroni Salad served as a snack on a summery hot day.

We have carefully selected a wide variety of Indian and Continental recipes in our main course section ranging from the delicious Masaledar Parathe to the exotic Italian Shell Pasta with Mushroom Sauce.

The valuable tips mentioned in every section will also guide you and make the whole cooking rigmarole a whole lot easier and quicker for you!

The purpose of this book is to delight you, working people, with a quick hearty meal and allow you to spend some much needed 'quality time' with your family and friends.

All in all, this is just a simple book to help make cooking an easy and enjoyable experience for you!

Happy cooking!!

Tarla Dalal

CONTENTS

Become a Quick Chef 9

A Few Time-saving Tips 11

Relationship between Tsp, Tbsp and Cups 12

Measuring Liquids 12

Trendy Garnishes 13

✠ SOUPS

Green Peas Soup 17

French Onion Soup 18

Creamy Vegetable Soup 20

Sweet Corn Soup 21

Thai Vegetable Soup 22

Man Chow Soup 24

✠ SALADS

Fig and Almond Salad 26

Herbal Macaroni Salad 27

Potato and Chana Salad 28

Dill Cucumber Salad 29

Garden Salad 30

✠ MAIN DISHES

Indian

Masaledar Parathe 32

Baby Corn Paneer Jalfrazie 34

Peshawari Subzi 36

Masala Masoor Dal 38

Spinach Pulao 39

Corn Pulao 40

Basic Gravies 41

Western

Vegetable Au Gratin 46

Shell Pasta with Creamy Mushroom Sauce 48

Foil Baked Buttered Rice with Mushroom Sauce 50

Mexican Rice 51

Saffron Rice with Broccoli Sauce .. 52

✠ SNACKS

Jhat-Pat Chaat.................. 56

Rice and Corn Croquettes 58

Creamy Corn Crackers 60

Stuffed French Rolls 62

Quick Spinach Pizzas 64

Quick Tomato Pizzas 67

Cheesy Puffs 69

Carrot and Cheese Fingers 70

Semolina Waffles 71

Mexican Bread Tartlets 73

Baked Beans Bread Tartlets 74

Satay Sticks 76

Crusty Potato Fingers 78

Spicy Paneer Fritters 79

Tasty Pav Bhaji Burgers 81

✠ DESSERTS

Fresh Fruit Gateau 84

Tiramisu Sundaé 87

Quick Chocolate Mousse Cake ... 89

Hot Fruit Salad with Vanilla
Ice-cream 91

Fruit Toppings for Vanilla
Ice-cream 92

Fresh Mango Ice-cream 96

Kaju Kopra Sheera 98

✠ BASIC RECIPES

How to Cook Pasta 100

Steamed Rice 101

Bread Tartlets 102

BECOME A QUICK CHEF

Successful meal preparation is dependent as much on planning as on cooking skills. Here are a few golden rules for time management.

1. The first step is to read the recipes thoroughly before making a menu. If you choose 2 or more hot dishes, consider their cooking times and oven temperatures. If you have only one oven and the temperatures required for the 2 dishes are different, this will present difficulties.

2. Next, make a shopping list. Check that you have all the ingredients you require. Once you have everything on hand, you can start the preparation.

3. Read through each recipe again so you know what lies ahead and try to estimate how long each preparation stage will take.

4. It is usually the case that most of the cooking has to be done at the same time, but we have only one pair of hands. So decide what can wait and what has to be done immediately. Grind masalas and pastes in advance.

5. Start with dishes that take the longest cooking time, setting time and work your way backwards i.e. the dessert for example, can be started just while you pressure cook the dal, then cook the vegetables. Prepare the salad and finally the parathas. If any recipe requires the oven to be pre-heated, do this first. Water for cooking of vegetables can be brought to a boil while you are doing the chopping and slicing.

6. Set out all the ingredients required and prepare them as specified in the recipe. If more than one dish calls for the same ingredients (example chopped onions) you can prepare the total amount at the same time.

7. Always use sharp knives. They will assist you in cutting and chopping quickly.

8. Use labour saving devices like a food processor, pressure cooker, a peeler, an electric whisk etc. that will make your job easier and quicker in the kitchen.

A FEW TIME-SAVING TIPS

1. When you are in a hurry choose ingredients like paneer, sweet corn kernels, bean sprouts etc. while cooking as these require less time to cook. Also use faster cooking methods like stir- frying and microwaving as compared to boiling and baking in the oven.

2. Remember to cut the vegetables into small pieces to enable faster cooking.

3. It is always handy to keep the following things in your refrigerator.
   a. **Boiled mixed vegetables:** These can be used to rustle up delicious subzis in just a few minutes.
   b. **Boiled potatoes:** Potatoes are very versatile and can be used in lots of recipes.
   c. **Pastes:** Onion paste, garlic paste, ginger paste, green chilli paste etc. last for a long time and can be used as required
   d. **Gravies:** Like tomato based gravy and white gravy should be made in bulk and frozen. These last for upto two months and help optimize on time. Refer for recipes kadai gravy, pg 41, white gravy, pg 42, makhani gravy, pg 44.

4. Innovative use of ready food mixes helps to shorten an elaborate recipe e.g. A sponge cake can be made using a cake mix. It can then be decorated with different kinds of icing to make a mouth - watering gateau.

RELATIONSHIP BETWEEN TEASPOON, TABLESPOON AND CUPS

1 tablespoon (15 ml.) = 3 teaspoons (5 ml. each)

3 tablespoons = ¼ cup

4 tablespoons + 1 teaspoon = ⅓ cup

6 tablespoons = ½ cup

8 tablespoons = ⅔ cup

13 tablespoons = 1 cup

MEASURING LIQUIDS

¼ teaspoon = 1.25 ml

½ teaspoon = 2.5 ml

1 teaspoon = 5 ml

1 tablespoon = 3 teaspoons = 15 ml

¼ cup = 50 ml

⅓ cup = 80 ml

½ cup = 100 ml

¾ cup = 150 ml

1 cup = 200 ml

TRENDY GARNISHES

One old saying about food that still rings true is: "*You eat with your eyes first.*" A simple touch of garnish can turn a dull dish into a wonderful one. Garnishes add eye appeal and beauty to almost any food. Garnishing the plate is one of the most important parts of cooking. Our appetite for a great meal is enhanced by its appearance. Most often, it is wise to garnish with something that is edible and blends with the flavour of the dish. A general rule of thumb about garnishes is to try and use an ingredient that's already in the dish. For example, simple chocolate curls placed on top of a dessert like a Quick Chocolate Mousse Cake, pg 89 adds to its beauty.

The garnish should enhance the flavour of the food and not detract from the dish in any way.

A Few Helpful Pointers

Always garnish food at the last minute to keep it looking fresh and inviting. Here are a few ideas:

- ✠ Give fresh herb leaves pizazz by dipping them into cold water. These make attractive garnishes.

- Make a chiffonade of greens to garnish rice and vegetables. To do this stack the leaves of greens such as lettuce, spinach, or cabbage, roll them into a cigar shape and then thinly slice crosswise. The resulting "ribbons" of green will make a colorful and flavourful garnish.

- Bundle several sprigs of different herbs together and place that bundle on the plate.

- For Mexican inspired dishes, you can slice tortillas into thin sticks and fry them in hot oil as a garnish. Likewise you can fry spinach for a similar, yet striking garnish.

- Curls of processed cheese are perfect on the top of a fresh veggie salad.

- Use fresh strawberries with the green tops still attached. Slice from the tip almost all the way to the stem end; carefully fan out the berry slices to make strawberry fans.

- Cut an X on the base of each cherry tomato. Using a sharp knife, carefully peel back the skin partway down the side of the tomato to make four petals of an edible tomato rose.

- Draw a fork lengthwise down a peeled cucumber; repeat all around vegetable. Cut cross-wise into slices for fluted cucumbers.

- Using a vegetable peeler, cut thin lengthwise strips of carrot. Roll each carrot strip and secure, with a wooden pick. Place in ice water for several hours to curl. Just before garnishing, remove wooden picks for fabulous carrot curls.

- Using a melon scooper, cut cucumbers into balls and arrange them to look like grape clusters, adding fresh herbs or celery leaves as the stem at top.

- Slice a thin piece of lemon about $1/8^{th}$ inch thick. Place it flat on your cutting board and insert the tip of your knife in the center. Pull the knife toward the edge, cutting a slit in the slice. Twist the ends on either side of the slit in opposite directions to form a twist.

- Peel a long strip of an orange or lemon peel using a zester. Tape one end to a straw then wrap the peel around it in a spiral and tape the other end. Freeze until set. To use these citrus spirals, cut away the area touched by the tape and remove the straw.

These are a few of our ideas but be inventive! Anything that you can eat, can easily morph into an eye-appealing garnish.

Soups

On a cold winter day, these piping hot steaming bowlfuls are as welcome as paradise itself.

Moreover this pre-meal food is a favourite with dieters and foodies alike. You could try serving light soups when serving heavy meals. A heavy soup is a meal by itself. Appropriate garnishes and accompaniments like warmed buttered bread rolls, croutons and bread sticks add to the enjoyment of the soup. The addition of a little cream tends to improve the taste of most soups. Never over-boil soups as they lose their colour and body. Lastly, always serve soups piping hot.

GREEN PEAS SOUP

✠ Preparation time : 10 minutes. ✠ Cooking time : 10 minutes. ✠ Serves 6.

2 cups green peas
½ cup chopped onions
1 cup white sauce, page 58
2 tbsp butter
salt and freshly crushed pepper to taste

For serving
fresh cream
bread croutons

1. Heat the butter in a pressure cooker and add the onions to it.
2. When the onions turn translucent, add the green peas and 1 cup of water and pressure cook till the peas are tender.
3. Blend to a smooth paste in a mixer. Strain.
4. Add the white sauce, salt and pepper and mix thoroughly.
   Serve hot topped with fresh cream and bread croutons.

Handy Tip: Bread crutons are made by cutting the bread into small cubes and deep- frying them in hot oil till crisp.

FRENCH ONION SOUP

Picture on facing page.

✠ Preparation time : 10 minutes. ✠ Cooking time : 10 minutes. ✠ Serves 6.
✠ Grilling time : 2 to 3 minutes.

1 cup thinly sliced onions
5 tbsp grated cheese (preferably cooking cheese)
2 slices bread
2 tbsp butter
salt to taste

1. Heat the butter in a pan and fry the onions on a very slow flame until brown in colour.
2. Add 5 cups of water, 3 tbsp of the grated cheese, and salt and boil for a few minutes.
3. Toast the bread slices in an oven at 150°C (300°F) or in a toaster till golden brown.
4. Butter lightly and sprinkle a little cheese on top. Cut each toast into 3 equal pieces.
5. Pour the soup into individual soup bowls, put a piece of toast in each bowl and sprinkle the remaining cheese on top of the toast.
6. Place below a hot grill , approximately 200°C (400°F) for a few minutes until the cheese starts sizzling.
   Serve hot.

FRENCH ONION SOUP : Recipe above →

CREAMY VEGETABLE SOUP

Picture on back cover.

✠ Preparation time : 10 minutes. ✠ Cooking time : 10 minutes. ✠ Serves 6.

1½ cups chopped mixed vegetables (french beans, carrots, green peas)
½ cup chopped onions
1½ tbsp plain flour (maida)
2½ cups milk
2 tbsp butter
salt to taste

For serving
grated cheese

1. Heat the butter in a pan and sauté the onions for 1 minute.
2. Add the flour and vegetables and sauté again for 2 to 3 minutes.
3. Add 2 cups of water and salt and cook until the vegetables are soft.
4. Add the milk and allow the soup to simmer for 2 to 3 minutes.
   Serve hot topped with the grated cheese.

SWEET CORN SOUP

✠ Preparation time : 10 minutes. ✠ Cooking time : 5 minutes. ✠ Serves 6.

1 can (450 gms) cream style corn
½ tsp soya sauce
2 tbsp cornflour, dissolved in ¼ cup of water
salt to taste

For serving
green chillies in vinegar
chilli sauce
soya sauce

1. Mix all the ingredients with 3 cups of water and bring to a boil.
2. Serve hot with chillies in vinegar, chilli sauce and soya sauce.

Handy tips : 1. Always keep a few cans of cream style corn handy so that you can make corn soup and other snacks in a few minutes.
2. Add ½ cup finely chopped vegetables like carrots, french beans, capsicum to make Vegetable Sweet Corn Soup. Remember that the cooking time will increase as all the vegetables have to be cooked.

THAI VEGETABLE SOUP

✠ Preparation time : 10 to 15 minutes. ✠ Cooking time : 15 minutes. ✠ Serves 6.

For the Thai vegetable stock
2 litres water
6 peppercorns
1 cup roughly chopped onions
2 cups chopped carrots
2 whole lemon grass stalks (hare chai ki patti), washed and chopped
salt to taste

Other ingredients
½ cup tofu or paneer (cottage cheese), cut into small cubes
½ cup chopped spring onions
½ cup sliced mushrooms
½ cup chopped coriander
½ cup shredded spinach (palak)
½ cup sliced and blanched baby corn
1 cup bean sprouts
2 tbsp green chillies in vinegar

10 flakes garlic, chopped
2 tbsp soya sauce
chilli powder to taste
1 tbsp butter

For the Thai vegetable stock
1. In a pot, simmer all the ingredients till they release their flavours. This should take about 10 to 15 minutes.
2. Strain and keep aside the liquid.

How to proceed
1. Heat the butter and sauté the spring onions and garlic. When onions turn translucent, add all the other ingredients and sauté for 3 to 4 minutes.
2. Add the Thai vegetable stock and bring it to a boil. Serve hot.

MAN CHOW SOUP

✠ Preparation time : 15 minutes. ✠ Cooking time : 10 minutes. ✠ Serves 4.

4½ cups clear vegetable stock or water with 1 seasoning cube
2 tbsp finely chopped tomatoes
2 tbsp finely chopped capsicum
2 tbsp finely chopped cauliflower
2 tbsp finely chopped carrots
2 tbsp finely chopped cabbage
2 tsp finely chopped garlic
2 tsp chopped ginger
1 tbsp fresh finely chopped mint (phudina) leaves
1 tbsp chopped coriander
3 tsp soya sauce
2 tbsp cornflour dissolved in ½ cup water
1 tbsp oil
salt and freshly crushed pepper to taste

1. Heat the oil in a wok or kadai over a high flame. Add the garlic, ginger, vegetables and stir-fry for 2 to 3 minutes over a high flame.
2. Add the stock, mint, coriander, soya sauce, salt and pepper.
3. Add the cornflour paste to the soup and boil for 1 minute. Serve hot.

Handy Tip: To make a clear vegetable stock quickly, just add roughly cut carrots, onions and celery to a vesselful of water and boil for about 15 minutes. Strain and use the liquid as required.

Salads

Salads can be served at the start of a meal or even as a complete meal by themselves. Today salads have no limitations. You need not even follow a fixed recipe to make a salad all the time. Let your taste buds guide you into making what you like. These are no longer considered food for the health conscious or the sick. Any salad tastes better and crisp if vegetables have been soaked in chilled water for a while. Never sprinkle salt in advance as the salad turns limp. For that extra crunch chill and then serve salads.

FIG AND ALMOND SALAD

✠ Preparation time : 5 minutes. ✠ No cooking. ✠ Serves 4.

6 firm fresh figs
2 cucumbers, cut into cubes
2 apples, cut into cubes
¼ cup blanched, peeled and sliced almonds
4 tbsp chopped mint leaves
1 cup lettuce leaves, torn into pieces

To be mixed into a dressing
2 tsp lemon juice
2 tsp sugar
2 to 3 drops almond essence
salt and freshly crushed pepper to taste

Combine all the ingredients and toss well with the dressing.
Serve immediately.

Handy tip: Dried figs that have been soaked overnight can be used when fresh figs are not in season.

HERBAL MACARONI SALAD

✠ Preparation time : 5 minutes. ✠ Cooking time : 5 minutes ✠ Serves 4.

1½ cups cooked fusilli, page 100
4 cups iceburg lettuce, torn into pieces
½ cup broccoli florets, blanched
¼ cup dried mushrooms, soaked
in lukewarm water
4 to 6 asparagus, cut into pieces, blanched
4 cherry tomatoes, halved

To be mixed into a dressing
¼ cup thick fresh curds (dahi)
½ cup cream
4 tbsp finely chopped spring
onion greens
2 tbsp finely chopped celery
a pinch of sugar
salt to taste

1. Drain and discard the water in which the mushrooms had been soaked.
2. Combine all the ingredients including the mushrooms in a large bowl and chill.
3. Just before serving, add the dressing and toss the salad well.
   Serve immediately.

Handy tips : 1. You can use any vegetable combination of your choice eg. baby corn, snow peas, carrots etc.
   2. After you blanch the vegetables, immerse them in cold water so that they retain their original colour.

POTATO AND CHANA SALAD

✠ Preparation time : 10 minutes. ✠ No cooking. ✠ Serves 6 to 8.

1½ cups boiled chick peas (Kabuli chana)
2 boiled potatoes, cut into pieces
½ cup paneer (cottage cheese) cubes
2 spring onions, chopped
2 tomatoes, chopped
½ tsp lemon juice
½ tsp finely chopped green chillies
1 tsp chaat masala
2 tsps chunda (sweet raw mango pickle)
1 tbsp chopped coriander
salt to taste

1. Mix all the ingredients very well.
2. Store in a refrigerator.
   Serve chilled.

DILL CUCUMBER SALAD

✠ Preparation time : 10 minutes. ✠ No cooking. ✠ Serves 4.

1½ cups sliced green cucumber
2 tbsp vinegar
¼ cup finely chopped fresh dill (suva bhaji)
1 boiled potato, peeled and cubed
¾ cup sliced onions
¾ cup peeled and sliced radish
¾ cup garlic mayonnaise
salt and freshly crushed peppercons to taste

1. Toss the cucumber slices in vinegar and salt and keep refrigerated for a 3 to 4 hours.
2. Drain and discard the liquid.
3. Add all the remaining ingredients to the marinated cucumber and toss well. Serve chilled.

GARDEN SALAD

Picture on page 2.

✠ Preparation time : 20 minutes. ✠ No cooking. ✠ Serves 6.

For the salad
½ cup watermelon cubes / scoops
½ cup pineapple cubes
½ cup black grapes
½ cup green cucumber slices
½ cup apple cubes
½ cup orange segments, peeled
7 to 8 mint (phudina) leaves

To be mixed into a creamy dressing
¾ cup thick fresh curds (dahi)
3 tbsp fresh cream
3 tbsp tomato ketchup
½ tsp chilli sauce
2 tbsp finely chopped onions
2 tbsp finely chopped capsicum
¼ tsp finely chopped green chillies
1 tsp mustard (rai) powder
1 tsp sugar
salt and freshly crushed peppercorns to taste

1. Mix all the ingredients for the salad and store in the refrigerator.
2. Serve chilled with the dressing.

Main Dishes

Make mouth-watering combinations from this wide array of Indian, Continental and fusion recipes. How about trying out our nutritious Peshawari Subzi with piping hot Masaledar Parathe or our delicious Saffron Rice with Broccoli Sauce. I'm sure you would have your family eating right out of your hands!!

Indian

MASALEDAR PARATHE

✠ Preparation time : 15 minutes. ✠ Cooking time : 20 minutes. ✠ Makes 8 parathas.

For the dough
1½ cups plain flour (maida)
½ cup milk
2 tsp melted butter
½ tsp salt
milk for making dough
plain flour (maida) for rolling
melted ghee for cooking

For the stuffing
1½ cups finely chopped mixed boiled
vegetables (french beans, carrots, green peas)
1 onion, chopped
1 potato, boiled
2 green chillies, chopped
½ tsp chilli powder
2 pinches garam masala
2 tbsp chopped coriander
2 tbsp ghee
salt to taste

For the dough
1. Sieve the flour with the salt. Mix all the ingredients with enough milk to make a soft dough.
2. Divide the dough into 8 portions. Keep aside.

For the stuffing
1. Heat the ghee in a pan and sauté the onion for 1 minute.
2. Add the remaining ingredients and cook for a few minutes. Add a little water if the mixture is dry.
3. Cool the mixture. Keep aside.

How to proceed
1. Roll each dough portion into a big thin round using a little plain flour for dusting.
2. Cook on a tava (griddle) on both sides for a few seconds.
3. Put some stuffing in the centre and fold like an envelope.
4. Cook on a tava (griddle) using a little ghee until both sides are golden brown in colour.
   Serve hot with chilled curds.

BABY CORN PANEER JALFRAZIE

✠ Preparation time : 10 minutes. ✠ Cooking time : 10 minutes. ✠ Serves 4.

12 no baby corn, cut into 4 lengthwise
1¼ cup paneer (cottage cheese), cut into 25 mm. (1") strips
3 spring onions whites, sliced
½ green capsicum, sliced
½ yellow capsicum, sliced
½ red capsicum, sliced
¼ tsp turmeric powder (haldi)
½ tsp chilli powder
½ tsp coriander-cumin seed (dhania-jeera) powder
1 tomato, sliced
2 tbsp tomato ketchup
2 tbsp tomato purée
3 spring onions greens, chopped
2 tsp vinegar
½ tsp garam masala
¼ tsp sugar
2 tbsp chopped coriander

1 tbsp oil
salt to taste

1. Heat the oil in a pan and add the spring onion whites and all the capsicum and sauté for 2 minutes.
2. Add the baby corn, turmeric powder, chilli powder, coriander- cumin seed powder, tomato, tomato ketchup, tomato purée and salt and sauté on a slow flame for 4 to 5 minutes till the baby corn is cooked.
3. Add the paneer, spring onion greens, vinegar, garam masala and sugar and toss lightly. Garnish with the chopped coriander and serve hot.

PESHAWARI SUBZI

Picture on facing page.

✠ Preparation time : 15 minutes. ✠ Cooking time : 8 minutes. ✠ Serves 6.

2 cups cubed and boiled vegetables (french beans, carrots, green peas, potatoes)
3 tbsp fresh cream
3 tbsp milk
2 tbsp oil
salt to taste

To be ground into a paste
2 onions, roughly chopped
4 green chillies
4 cloves garlic
12 mm. (½") piece ginger
2 cardamoms (elaichi)

1. Heat the oil in a pan and fry the paste for 2 minutes.
2. Add the vegetables, cream, milk and salt and cook for a few minutes, till the gravy thickens.
   Serve hot with parathas.

PESHAWARI SUBZI : Recipe above ↪

MASALA MASOOR DAL

Picture on cover.

✠ Preparation time : 20 minutes. ✠ Cooking time : 20 minutes. ✠ Serves 6.

1 cup masoor dal (split red lentils), soaked for 30 minutes and washed
1 cup chopped mixed boiled vegetables (french beans, carrots, green peas, potatoes)
1 onion, chopped
1 tsp cumin seeds (jeera)
2 tsp amchur (dry mango) powder
1 tomato, chopped
½ tsp turmeric powder (haldi)
¼ tsp chilli powder
2 tbsp ghee
salt to taste

To be ground into a paste
6 cloves garlic
6 green chillies
25 mm. (1") piece ginger

1. Pressure cook the dal with 1½ cups of water.
2. Heat the ghee in a saucepan, add the onions and cumin seeds and sauté for at least 2 minutes.
3. Add the cooked dal, boiled vegetables, amchur powder, tomato, turmeric powder, paste and salt. Boil for a few minutes.
4. Just before serving, heat the ghee in a small pan, add the chilli powder and pour over the dal mixture. Serve hot.

SPINACH PULAO

✠ Preparation time : 15 minutes. ✠ Cooking time : 5 minutes. ✠ Serves 6.
✠ Baking time : 15 minutes. ✠ Baking temperature : 200°C (400°F).

For the rice
3 cups steamed rice, page 101
½ cup milk
2 tbsp butter
salt to taste

For the spinach
2 cups chopped spinach (palak)
½ tsp cumin seeds (jeera)
1 onion, chopped
1 green chilli, chopped
2 tbsp oil
salt to taste

Other ingredients
butter for greasing

For the rice
Heat the butter in a pan on a slow flame and add the steamed rice, milk and salt. Cook for 1 minute. Keep a aside.

For the spinach
1. Heat the oil and fry the cumin seeds until they begin to crackle. Add the onions and fry for 1 minute. Add the green chilli and fry again for a few seconds.
2. Add the spinach and salt and cook until soft.

How to proceed
1. Spread the spinach at the bottom of a greased jelly mould.
2. Spread the rice on top. Press well and cover.
3. Bake in a pre-heated oven at 200°C (400°F) for 10 minutes.
4. While serving, invert on a plate and serve hot with a kadhi of your choice.

VARIATION: Corn Pulao
> Use 1½ cups of cooked tender corn kernels instead of spinach.

BASIC GRAVIES

To make a subzi, just heat about ½ cup of any of these gravies, add 2 cups of boiled mixed vegetables and salt and cook for 8-10 minutes. Water may be added as required and fresh cream to make it richer.

KADAI GRAVY

✠ Preparation time : 10 minutes. ✠ Cooking time: 15 to 20 minutes. ✠ Makes 2 cups.

750 gms tomatoes
1 tbsp coriander (dhania) seeds
10 whole dry red chillies, broken into pieces
6 cloves garlic, chopped
4 green chillies, chopped
50 mm. (2") piece ginger, grated
1 tsp kasoori methi (dried fenugreek leaves)
1 tsp garam masala
4 tbsp oil
salt to taste

1. Roast the coriander seeds and red chillies lightly on a tava (griddle) and pound with a mortar and pestle to crush them.
2. Heat the oil in a pan, add the garlic and sauté over medium heat for a few minutes.
3. Add the pounded spices and cook for a few seconds.
4. Add the green chillies and ginger and sauté for 30 seconds.
5. Add the tomatoes and fry until the oil comes to the surface.
6. Add the kasuri methi and salt and sprinkle garam masala.
7. Cool and freeze in an air-tight container or in polythene bags.

WHITE GRAVY

✠ Preparation time : 10 minutes. ✠ Cooking time: 15 minutes. ✠ Makes 2 cups.

2 medium onions, roughly chopped
1 tbsp broken cashewnuts
6 cloves garlic, roughly chopped
12 mm. (½") piece ginger
3 green cardamoms (elaichi)
2 cloves (laung)

1 bay leaf (tejpatta)
2 green chillies, chopped
1 cup fresh curds (dahi)
1 tbsp fresh cream
2 tbsp oil
salt to taste

1. Cut the onions into big pieces.
2. Add ¾ cup of water and boil. When cooked, add the cashewnut pieces, garlic and ginger. Leave aside to cool.
3. When cool, blend to a smooth paste in the blender.
4. Heat the oil in a pan and add the cardamoms, cloves and bay leaf and stir for about ½ minute.
5. Add the onion-ginger paste and fry for 1 minute.
6. Add the green chillies and fry for a while. Remove from the heat.
7. Add the curds. Mix well and cook for ½ minute, stirring continuously. Add the cream and salt.
8. Cool and freeze in an air-tight container or in polythene bags.

MAKHNI GRAVY

✠ Preparation time : 15 minutes. ✠ Cooking time: 20 minutes. ✠ Makes 2 cups.

1 cup chopped onions
25 mm. (1") piece ginger
6 to 7 cloves garlic
2 tbsp broken cashewnuts
1 tsp chilli powder
2 cups fresh tomato purée
1 tsp cumin seed (jeera) powder
½ tsp garam masala
1 tsp kasuri methi (dried fenugreek seeds)
1 tbsp honey
¼ cup milk
¼ cup cream
1 tbsp oil
1 tbsp butter
salt to taste

1. Blend the onions, ginger, garlic and cashewnuts to a smooth paste in a mixer.

2. Heat the oil in a pan, add the ground paste and cook till it is light brown in colour.
3. Add the chilli powder and tomato purée and cook for a few minutes.
4. Add the cumin seed powder, garam masala and ½ cup of water and cook for some time till the oil separates from the masala. Keep aside.
5. In another pan, melt the butter, add the kasuri methi and remove from flame.
6. Add this to the tomato gravy, along with the honey, milk, cream and salt and allow it to come to a boil.
7. Cool and freeze in an air-tight container or in polythene bags.

Western

VEGETABLE AU GRATIN

✠ Preparation time : 20 minutes. ✠ Cooking time : 10 minutes ✠ Serves 4.
✠ Baking time : 15 to 20 minutes. ✠ Baking temperature : 200°C (400°F).

1½ cups chopped mixed bolied vegetables (carrots, peas, broccoli, zucchini, baby corn, french beans)
½ cup paneer (cottage cheese) cubes
1 tsp oil

For the white sauce
2 tbsp refined flour (maida)
1½ cups milk
¼ cup grated cheese
½ tsp grated garlic
½ tsp red chilli flakes (paprika)
2 tbsp butter
salt and pepper to taste

For the topping
½ cup grated cheese
½ cup bread crumbs

For serving
garlic bread

For the white sauce
1. Heat the butter in a pan and sauté the garlic and chilli flakes for 1 to 2 seconds.
2. Add the flour and sauté for 2 to 3 minutes.
3. Add the milk gradually stirring continuously so that lumps do not form, add ½ cup of water and mix well.
4. Bring to a boil and add the cheese, salt and pepper and mix well.

How to proceed
1. Sauté the paneer cubes in oil on a non stick pan till they are lightly browned.
2. Combine the vegetables and the white sauce and mix well.
3. Pour into an oven-proof bowl and sprinkle the cheese and bread crumbs on top.
4. Bake in a pre-heated oven at 200°C (400°F) for 10 to 15 minutes till the cheese melts and is lightly browned.
Serve with warm garlic bread.

SHELL PASTA WITH CREAMY MUSHROOM SAUCE

✠ Preparation time : 15 minutes. ✠ Cooking time : 15 minutes. ✠ Serves 4.

3 cups cooked shell pasta (conchiglie), page 100

For the mushroom sauce
3 cups thickly sliced mushrooms
1 cup sliced onions
2 tsp chopped garlic
2 tbsp plain flour (maida)
3 cups milk
¼ cup fresh cream
5 tbsp butter
salt and freshly crushed peppercorns to taste

For the garnish
½ cup grated cheese

For the mushroom sauce
1. Heat the butter in a large saucepan, add the onions and garlic and cook for some time.
2. Add the mushrooms and flour and cook for a further 3 to 4 minutes.
3. Add the milk gradually, mixing well to make sure no lumps form. Bring to a boil.
4. Add the fresh cream, salt and pepper and keep aside.

How to proceed
Just before serving, re-heat the sauce, adding a little milk or water if required and toss the pasta in it.
Serve hot garnished with the grated cheese.

Handy tip : If you like, brandy can be added at step 4 to flavour this sauce.

FOIL BAKED BUTTERED RICE WITH MUSHROOM SAUCE

✠ Preparation time : 5 minutes. ✠ Cooking time : 5 minutes. ✠ Serves 6.
✠ Baking time : 15 to 20 minutes. ✠ Baking Temperature : 200°C (400°F).

1 recipe steamed rice, page 101
1 recipe mushroom sauce, page 48
3 tbsp butter
½ tsp salt

1. Heat 2 tbsp of butter in a pan on a slow flame and add the cooked rice and salt and cook for 1 minute.
2. Place some buttered rice in aluminum foil. Spread some mushroom sauce over it.
3. Make similar layers using the remaining rice and mushroom sauce.
4. Dot with the remaining butter and make a parcel, leaving enough room for expansion of the steam generated while cooking.
5. Cook on a hot charcoal sigri grill for 10 to 15 minutes, turning the parcel a couple of times while cooking. Alternatively, bake in a hot oven at 200°C (400°F) for 10 to 15 minutes. Serve hot.

MEXICAN RICE

Picture on page 75.

✠ Preparation time : 15 minutes. ✠ Cooking time : 5 minutes. ✠ Serves 6.

3 cups steamed rice, page 101
1 onion, chopped
2 tsp red chilli flakes (paprika)
4 cloves garlic
1½ cups mixed boiled vegetables (french beans, carrots, cauliflower, potatoes, corn)
½ cup soaked and cooked rajma (kidney beans)
salt to taste

1. Pound the red chilli flakes and garlic in a mortar-pestle.
2. Heat the oil in a pan, add the onions and sauté for 2 minutes. Add the paste and sauté again for 1 minute.
3. Add the chilli powder, vegetables and rajma and sauté for 2 minutes.
4. Add the rice and salt. Mix well.
   Serve hot.

SAFFRON RICE WITH BROCCOLI SAUCE

Picture on page 1.

✠ Preparation time : 15 minutes. ✠ Cooking time : 25 minutes. ✠ Serves 6.

For the saffron rice
3 cups steamed rice, page 101
4 tbsp milk
2 pinches saffron (kesar)
1 tbsp chopped dill (optional)
1 tbsp butter
salt to taste

For the broccoli sauce
1 cup chopped fresh broccoli
¾ cup finely chopped onions
½ tsp finely chopped green chilli
1 tbsp cornflour
2 pinches oregano (optional)
¾ cup milk
2 tbsp butter
salt to taste

For the saffron rice
1. Heat the butter in a pan on a slow flame, add the rice and milk and mix well.
2. Prepare the saffron by rubbing in a little warm milk. Add to the rice.
3. Add the dill and salt and cook for 2 to 3 minutes. Keep aside.

For the broccoli sauce
1. Put the broccoli in salted boiling water for 2 minutes.
2. Heat the butter in a pan and fry the onions and green chilli for ½ minute.
3. Add the broccoli and cook for 2 to 3 minutes.
4. Mix the cornflour in the milk and ¾ cup of water and add to the broccoli.
5. Add the oregano and cook for a few minutes or until the mixture thickens, while stirring continuously.
6. Add salt and mix well. Keep aside.

How to proceed
1. Fill a greased ring mould with the hot rice and invert on a serving plate.
2. Fill the centre with broccoli sauce.
   Serve hot.

Snacks

Try these simple but creative snacks. There is a wide variety to choose from. For a party or a get together it will pay to make appetizers and snacks well in advance. Use cooking cheese (which melts easily) for snack toppings. Use appropriate garnishes like olive slices, capsicum, coriander leaves, etc. to appeal your guests.

JHAT-PAT CHAAT : Recipe on page 56 →

JHAT-PAT CHAAT

Picture on page 55.

✠ Preparation time : 30 minutes. ✠ Cooking time : 20 minutes. ✠ Serves 6 to 8.

¾ cup green peas
½ cup chick peas (Kabuli chana), soaked overnight
¼ cup white peas (dried), soaked overnight
½ cup moong sprouts, parboiled
3 potatoes, peeled and parboiled
¼ cup chopped tomatoes
¼ cup chopped onions
sweet chutney to taste
green chutney to taste
chilli garlic chutney to taste
salt to taste
oil for deep frying

For the garnish
¼ cup nylon sev

¼ cup chopped coriander
¼ cup raw mango slices

1. Boil the peas, chick peas and white peas separately till tender.
2. Drain and keep aside.
3. Cut the potatoes into strips like french fries. Deep- fry in hot oil till golden brown and then drain on absorbent paper.
4. Mix all the ingredients together, and serve garnished with the sev, chopped coriander and raw mango.
   Serve hot.

RICE AND CORN CROQUETTES

✠ Preparation time : 20 minutes. ✠ Cooking time : 15 minutes.
✠ Makes 10 croquettes.

For the croquettes
1½ cups cooked tender corn
¾ cup cooked rice
1 tbsp chopped celery
4 chopped green chillies (optional)
salt to taste

For the white sauce
1½ cups milk
4 tbsp butter
5 tbsp plain flour (maida)
salt to taste

For the stuffing
2 tbsp grated cheese

Other ingredients
¼ cup plain flour (maida)
bread crumbs
oil for deep-frying

For serving
tomato ketchup

For the white sauce
1. Melt the butter in a pan on a slow flame. Add the flour and cook on a slow flame, while stirring throughout, until froth appears.

2. Add the milk gradually. Cook and stir continuously until the mixture becomes very thick. Add salt and mix well.
   Cool and keep aside.

For the croquettes
1. Crush the cooked corn slightly.
2. Mix the corn, rice, white sauce, celery, green chillies and salt.
3. Divide into 10 equal portions and shap each portion into flat rounds.
4. Put a little cheese in the centre and close very well.
5. Mould each cheese centred portion into a cylinder. Keep aside.
6. Just before serving, mix ½ cup of water with the plain flour.
7. Dip the croquettes into this paste, roll over bread crumbs and deep-fry in hot oil till golden brown.
   Serve hot with tomato ketchup.

CREAMY CORN CRACKERS

✠ Preparation time : 15 minutes. ✠ Grilling time: 5 to 10 minutes.
✠ Makes 25 pieces.

For the base
25 cream cracker biscuits

For the corn filling
1 can (450 gms) cream style corn
½ cup chopped onions
2 tbsp chopped carrots
2 tbsp chopped capsicums
1 green chilli, chopped
1 tsp lemon juice or vinegar
1 tbsp oil
salt to taste

For baking
grated cooking cheese

For serving
Tabasco sauce or chilli sauce

For the corn filling
1. Heat the oil in a pan, add the onions, carrots, capsicums and sauté and cook on a high flame for 2 to 3 minutes.
2. Add the green chilli and fry again for a few seconds.
3. Add the corn, lemon juice and salt and mix well.

How to proceed
1. Arrange the biscuits on a baking tray.
2. Spread some filling on each biscuit and sprinkle grated cheese on top.
3. Put under a hot grill for 3 to 4 minutes.
   Serve hot with Tobasco or chilli sauce.

Note: You can also use khari (puffed) biscuits instead of cream cracker biscuits but split them into two horizontally before spreading the filling (i.e. step 1 of how to proceed).

STUFFED FRENCH ROLLS

✠ Preparation time : 15 minutes. ✠ Cooking time : 5 minutes ✠ Serves 6 to 8.
✠ Baking time : 9 minutes. ✠ Baking temperature : 200°C (400°F).

For the French rolls
2 French rolls (12 " in length)
¼ cup grated cheese
2 tbsp melted butter

For the filling
1 cup chopped baby corn, blanched
½ cup chopped capsicum
½ cup finely chopped onions
½ green chilli, chopped
1½ cups white sauce, page 58
2 tbsp grated cheese
a few drops chilli sauce
1 tbsp butter
salt to taste

For the French rolls
1. Divide each roll horizontally into two parts. Scoop out the centres.
2. Brush the scooped sides with melted butter.
3. Bake in a pre-heated oven at 200°C (400°F) for 5 minutes.

For the filling
1. Heat the butter in a pan and sauté the onions and green chilli for 1 minute.
2. Add the baby corn and capsicum and fry again for a few minutes.
3. Add the white sauce and cheese and cook for 2 minutes.
4. Add the chilli sauce, salt and pepper. Mix well.

How to proceed
1. Spread a little filling in each bread half.
2. Cover with grated cheese.
3. Place under a hot grill for 4 to 5 minutes or until the cheese has melted.
4. Cut each roll into 3 to 4 pieces and serve hot.

QUICK SPINACH PIZZAS

Picture on facing page.

✠ Preparation time : 20 minutes. ✠ Cooking time : 15 minutes ✠ Makes 2 pizzas.
✠ Baking time : 15 minutes. ✠ Baking temperature : 200°C (400°F).

2 ready-made 8" pizza bases
oil for brushing

For the spinach filling
2½ cups chopped spinach (palak)
2 tbsp chopped onions
½ tsp chopped green chillies
1 tbsp fresh cream
¼ cup paneer (cottage cheese) cubes
1 tbsp oil or butter
salt and pepper to taste

QUICK TOMATO PIZZAS : Recipe on page 67, QUICK SPINACH PIZZAS : Recipe above →

For the topping
red, green, yellow capsicum slices
grated cooking cheese (preferably Mozzarella)

For the spinach filling
1. Cook the spinach in very little water until soft. Drain.
2. Heat the oil in a pan and fry the onions and green chillies for 1 minute.
3. Add the spinach, salt and pepper and cook for 1 minute.
4. Add the cream and paneer. Mix well.

How to proceed
1. Brush a tray with oil and arrange the pizza crusts on it.
2. Spread some spinach filling on each crust and place the capsicum slices on top.
3. Sprinkle some cheese and bake in a pre-heated oven at 200°C (400°F) for 10 minutes or until the cheese melts.
   Serve hot.

QUICK TOMATO PIZZAS

Picture on page 65.

✠ Preparation time : 10 minutes. ✠ Cooking time : 10 minutes ✠ Makes 2 pizzas.
✠ Baking time : 10 minutes. ✠ Baking temperature : 200°C (400°F).

2 ready-made (8") pizza bases
oil for brushing

For the tomato sauce
4 large tomatoes
1/3 cup finely chopped onions
1 tsp chopped garlic
¼ cup tomato ketchup
1 tsp sugar
½ tsp dried oregano
2 tbsp oil
salt to taste

Other ingredients
1 tbsp oil for cooking
1 cup grated cooking cheese
(preferably Mozzarella)
1 capsicum, cut into rings
1 tsp red chilli flakes (paprika)

For the tomato sauce
1. Blanch the tomatoes in boiling water.
2. Peel, cut into quarters and deseed the tomatoes.
3. Chop finely and keep the tomato pulp aside.
4. Heat the oil in a pan, add the onions and garlic and sauté for a few minutes.
5. Add the tomato pulp and allow it to simmer for 10 to 15 minutes until the sauce reduces a little.
6. Add the ketchup, sugar and salt and simmer for some more time.
7. Finally, add the oregano and mix well.

How to proceed
1. Brush a tray with oil and arrange the pizza crusts on it.
2. Spread some tomato sauce on each crust.
3. Arrange capsicum rings and sprinkle some cheese on the pizzas.
4. Bake in a pre-heated oven at 200°C (400°F) for 10 minutes or until the cheese has melted.
5. Sprinkle red chilli flakes on top and serve hot.

CHEESY PUFFS

✠ Preparation time : 15 minutes. ✠ Grilling time : 5 to 10 minutes. ✠ Makes 25 pieces.

For the base
25 mini khari biscuits (puff pastry biscuits)

For the filling
2 cups white sauce, page 58
1 green chilli, chopped
4 tbsp grated cooking cheese
salt and pepper to taste
½ tsp red chilli powder, for sprinkling

For the filling
Mix the white sauce, green chilli, 2 tbsp of cheese, salt and pepper.

How to proceed
1. Split each biscuit into 2 horizontally. On top of each half spread the filling and sprinkle the remaining cheese.
2. Sprinkle chilli powder on top and grill for a few minutes, till the cheese melts. Serve hot.

CARROT AND CHEESE FINGERS

✠ Preparation time : 10 minutes. ✠ Cooking time: 10 minutes. ✠ Serves 4.

2 carrots
1 cup grated cooking cheese
2 tbsp soft butter
2 tsp tomato ketchup
½ tsp Tabasco sauce
4 slices bread
salt to taste

For the garnish
tomato slices

1. Grate the carrots and mix with 4 to 5 tbsp of cheese, 1½ tbsp of butter, tomato ketchup, Tabasco sauce and salt.
2. Toast the bread slices and spread the remaining butter on top.
3. Pile the cheese and carrot mixture on the toasted slices.
4. Sprinkle the remaining cheese on top and put under the hot grill till the cheese melts.
5. Cut each toast into 3 fingers.
6. Garnish with the tomato slices and serve hot.

SEMOLINA WAFFLES

✠ Preparation time : 15 minutes. ✠ Cooking time: 20 to 30 minutes. ✠ Serves 4.

¾ cup semolina (rava)
¾ cup plain flour (maida)
5 tbsp fresh curds (dahi)
1 tsp baking powder
2 tbsp chopped coriander
½ cup chopped cabbage
2 tbsp cooked corn (optional)
a pinch asafoetida (hing)
1 tbsp oil
4 to 6 chopped green chillies
a pinch sugar (optional)

For serving
grated cheese
green chutney

1. Sieve the semolina and plain flour.
2. Add the curds, 2 to 3 tbsp of warm water and baking powder and mix into a batter. Keep aside.
3. After about 2 hours, add the remaining ingredients.
4. Pre-heat the waffle iron and pour ¾ cup of the mixture in the centre of the iron and close the lid. Bake for approx. 7 minutes, till the waffles are golden in colour.
5. Repeat with the rest of the batter to make more waffles.
   Serve hot with butter and grated cheese.

Handy tip : If you do not have a waffle iron, make pancakes on a tava (griddle).

MEXICAN BREAD TARTLETS

✠ Preparation time : 10 minutes. ✠ Cooking time : 5 minutes ✠ Makes 10 tartlets.
✠ Baking time : 10 to 15 minutes. ✠ Baking temperature : 200°C (400°F).

10 bread tartlets, page 102
2 cups cooked tender corn
1/3 cup chopped onions
1/4 cup chopped capsicum
2 tomatoes
3 tbsp grated cooking cheese
2 green chillies, finely chopped
3 tbsp oil
salt to taste

1. Put the tomatoes in hot water for 10 minutes. Take off the skin and chop them finely.
2. Heat the oil in pan and sauté the onions for 1 minute.
3. Add the capsicum, tomatoes and green chillies and sauté for at least 3 to 4 minutes.

4. Add the corn and salt.
5. In each tartlet case, fill a little mixture, spread a little tomato ketchup and sprinkle some cheese on top.
6. Bake in a pre-heated oven at 200°C (400°F) for 5 to 10 minutes or until the cheese melts.

   Serve hot.

VARIATION: Baked Beans Bread Tartlets

Add baked beans instead of the corn mixture.

MEXICAN RICE : Recipe on page 51 →

SATAY STICKS

✠ Preparation time : 10 minutes. ✠ Cooking time: 8 minutes. ✠ Serves 4.

½ cup paneer (cottage cheese), cut into 12 mm. (½") cubes
½ cup baby corn, cut into 25 mm. (1") pieces
½ green or red capsicum, cut into 12 mm. (½") cubes
1 tbsp oil

To be mixed into a marinade
2 tsp curry powder
2 tsp lemon juice
2 tsp honey
½ tsp salt
1 tbsp oil

For the peanut sauce
2 tbsp peanut butter
½ tsp soya sauce
1 tsp sugar

½ tsp chilli powder
salt to taste

For the peanut sauce
1. Combine all the ingredients in a pan with ½ cup of water. Mix well.
2. Bring the sauce to a boil. Remove and keep aside.

How to proceed
1. In a large bowl, combine the paneer, baby corn, capsicum and the prepared marinade and toss well.
2. Arrange a piece of paneer, capsicum and baby corn on a toothpick. Repeat for the remaining vegetables (to make approx. 15 sticks).
3. Heat the oil on a tava (griddle) and sauté the satay sticks on all sides till the vegetables brown lightly (approx. 4 to 5 minutes).
   Serve hot with the peanut sauce.

Handy Tip: Curry Powder is a dry spice blend that is available at provision stores.

CRUSTY POTATO FINGERS

✠ Preparation time : 15 minutes. ✠ Cooking time: 15 minutes. ✠ Serves 4.

2 medium sized potatoes, cut into fingers
finely crushed cornflakes or toasted bread crumbs (for coating)
oil for deep-frying

For the batter	**To be made into a paste (for the batter)**
¾ cup plain flour (maida)	1 onion, chopped
1 tbsp cornflour	2 green chillies, chopped
salt to taste	12 mm. (½") piece ginger
	salt to taste

1. Parboil the potatoes in salted water. Drain and keep aside.
2. Make a batter by mixing the plain flour, cornflour and salt.
3. Add the paste and enough water to make a thick batter.
4. Dip the potato fingers in the batter, roll out in the finely crushed corn flakes or toasted bread crumbs and deep-fry in hot oil on a medium flame till golden brown.
   Drain on absorbent paper and serve hot.

SPICY PANEER FRITTERS

✠ Preparation time : 5 minutes. ✠ Cooking time: 8 minutes. ✠ Makes 16 fritter.

1 cup crumbled paneer (cottage cheese)
1 tsp chilli powder
2 large cloves garlic, grated
2 tsp tomato ketchup
1 tsp cornflour
salt to taste
oil for deep-frying

For the covering
5 tbsp plain flour (maida)
6 samosa pattis, finely chopped

For serving
green chutney

1. Combine the paneer, chilli powder, garlic, tomato ketchup cornflour and salt and mix well.
2. Divide the mixture into 16 equal portions.
3. Shape each portion into a 37 mm. (1½") long cylindrical roll. Keep aside.
4. Make a batter using the plain flour and water.
5. Dip the prepared paneer rolls into the flour batter and then coat them in samosa patti pieces.
6. Deep fry the paneer fritters in hot oil, a few pieces at a time, till they are golden brown in colour.
7. Drain on absorbent paper.
   Serve hot with green chutney.

TASTY PAV BHAJI BURGERS

✠ Preparation time : 15 minutes. ✠ Cooking time : 10 minutes ✠ Makes 6 burgers.
✠ Baking time : 7 to 8 minutes. ✠ Baking temperature : 150°C (300°F).

For the burgers
6 small round burgers
butter for brushing

For the stuffing
2 potatoes, boiled and grated
1 cup boiled and chopped mixed vegetables (green peas and cauliflower)
½ cup chopped tomatoes
½ cup chopped onions
½ tsp chopped garlic
1 tbsp chopped capsicum
½ tsp chilli powder or red chilli paste
½ tsp pav bhaji masala
2 tbsp chopped coriander
a few drops of lemon juice
2 tbsp butter
salt to taste

For serving
onion rings

For the burgers
1. Divide the buns into two parts horizontally.
2. Brush them with the butter and bake in a pre-heated oven at 150°C (300°F) for a few minutes.

For the stuffing
1. Heat the butter in a pan and fry the onions and garlic for ½ minute.
2. Add the capsicum, tomatoes, chillies powder and pav bhaji masala and fry for at least 1 minute.
3. Add the potatoes and the vegetables, coriander, lemon juice and salt and cook for 2 minutes. If the mixture is too thick, sprinkle a little water.

How to proceed
1. Spread some pav bhaji mixture on the bottom portion of a burger, place some onion rings on top and cover it with the remaining top of the bun. Repeat with the remaining mixture and burgers to make 5 more pav bhaji burgers.
2. Brush with the butter and bake in a pre-heated oven at 150°C (300°F) for a few minutes.
   Serve hot.

 # Desserts

No meal is complete without a dessert. An elegant dessert rounds off the success of any dinner party. Keeping this in mind, here are some dessert recipes that are not only eggless but also gelatin free. Here's a quickie, when you are in a hurry, serve ice-cream in a tall glass topped with fruits and different sauces as a dessert and you are bound to impress your guests.

FRESH FRUIT GATEAU

Picture on facing page.

✠ Preparation time : 8 to 9 minutes. ✠ No cooking. ✠ Makes 1 gateau.

1 (150 mm. (6") diameter) white sponge

For the Chantilly cream
2 cups (250 grams) fresh cream
¼ cup powdered sugar
1 tsp vanilla essence

To be mixed into a soaking syrup
2 tbsp sugar
2 tbsp orange squash
¼ cup water

FRESH FRUIT GATEAU : Recipe above ↪

For the filling
1 cup sliced seasonal citrus fruits (orange, kiwis, strawberries, black grapes, peaches and pineapple)

For the garnish
few fruit slices
dark chocolate curls

For the Chantilly cream
1. Combine the cream, sugar and vanilla essence in a clean and dry bowl and whisk till soft peaks form.
2. Keep refrigerated till required.

How to proceed
1. Slice the cake horizontally into 2 equal layers and divide the cream into 2 equal portions.
2. Sprinkle the bottom layer of the sponge cake with ½ the soaking syrup.
3. Spread one portion of the Chantilly cream on the soaked layer of sponge.
4. Top with half the fruits and place another layer of sponge on it.
5. Sprinkle some more soaking syrup and then spread another portion of the Chantilly cream over this layer.
6. Garnish with the fruits and chocolate curls and refrigerate. Serve chilled.

TIRAMISU SUNDAÉ

✠ Preparation time : 10 minutes. ✠ No cooking. ✠ Makes 2 sundaés.

6 butter cookies
6 scoops coffee ice-cream
1 cup whipped cream

To be mixed into a soaking syrup
¼ cup water
1 tbsp powdered sugar
1 tbsp instant coffee granules
1 tbsp brandy or kahlua

For the garnish
1 tsp cocoa powder
1 tbsp chopped walnuts

1. Place the cookies in a dish and pour the soaking syrup over it.
2. Turn the cookies over once so that both sides are evenly soaked. Keep aside.
3. Place one scoop of ice-cream in a sundaé glass.

4. Top with a soaked cookie and then some whipped cream.
5. Top with 2 more scoops of ice-cream.
6. Add 2 more soaked cookies and top with some more whipped cream.
7. Serve immediately, garnished with a sprinkling of cocoa powder and chopped walnuts.
8. Repeat with the remaining ingredients to make another sundaé.

QUICK CHOCOLATE MOUSSE CAKE

✠ Preparation time : 8 minutes. ✠ Cooking time: 7 minutes. ✠ Serves 6 to 8.

1 (150 mm. (6") diameter) chocolate sponge cake
1 packet china grass (chocolate flavour)
2½ cups (500 ml.) milk
¼ cup cocoa powder
200 ml vanilla ice-cream

For the garnish
½ cup grated dark chocolate

1. Cut the cake horizontally into half. Put one half back into the tin.
2. Let the ice-cream soften a little by leaving it at room temperature for 10 minutes.
3. Heat the milk with the china grass, stirring till it dissolves. Add the cocoa powder. Heat for some more time. Strain and let it cool.
4. When the milk mixture comes to room temperature, whisk in the ice-cream.
5. Pour half this mixture over one half of the cake which is placed in the tin.

6. Place the other half of the cake on top and pour the remaining mixture on it.
7. Refrigerate till firm.
   Serve chilled garnished with the grated chocolate.

HOT FRUIT SALAD WITH VANILLA ICE-CREAM

✠ Preparation time : 15 minutes. ✠ Cooking time: 10 minutes. ✠ Serves 10 to 12.

2 cups canned mixed fruit (peach, pineapple, grapes, apple, chikoo etc.), sliced
2 tbsp sugar
1 cup orange juice
juice of 1 lemon
a little liqueur (optional)
1 to 2 tbsp brandy

1. Drain the fruit and keep aside the syrup from the can.
2. Add 1 tbsp of water to the sugar and heat gently until it has melted and begins to turn golden.
3. Add the orange juice and lemon juice and the fruit syrup. If you like, flavour with a little liqueur.
4. Add the drained fruit and cook for a few minutes.
5. Warm the brandy in a large spoon, set alight and pour the burning brandy over the fruit.
    Serve hot with vanilla ice-cream.

FRUIT TOPPINGS FOR VANILLA ICE-CREAM

Given below are recipes of some sauces. These can be made before and kept in the refrigerators. Served on top of Vanilla ice-cream, they make delightful desserts.

ORANGE SAUCE

✠ Preparation time: a few minutes. ✠ Cooking time: 5 minutes. ✠ Makes 1 cup.

¾ cup orange juice
2 tbsp orange squash
3 tsp sugar
2 tsp corn flour
a few drops edible orange colour
a few drops orange essence
½ tsp lemon juice

1. Mix the orange juice, orange squash, sugar and corn flour and cook until thick. Allow to cool.
2. Add the colour, essence and lemon juice. Mix well and use as required.

CHOCOLATE SAUCE

✠ Preparation time: 5 minutes. ✠ Cooking time: 5 minutes. ✠ Makes 1 cup.

2 tbsp grated chocolate
2 tbsp cocoa powder
2 tbsp brown sugar or plain sugar
2 tbsp corn flour
1 tbsp butter

Mix all the ingredients with 1½ cups of water and cook on a slow flame till the mixture is slightly thick. Use as required.

STRAWBERRY SAUCE

✠ Preparation time: 10 minutes. ✠ Cooking time: 10 minutes. ✠ Makes 2½ cups.

2 cups strawberry purée
3 tbsp granulated sugar
2 tbsp corn flour

2 tsp lemon juice
a few drops edible red colour

1. Mix the strawberry purée, sugar and corn flour and boil until the mixture becomes thick.
2. Blend in a liquidiser.
3. Add the lemon juice and red colour. Use as required.

MANGO SAUCE

✠ Preparation time: 10 minutes. ✠ Cooking time: 10 minutes. ✠ Makes 2½ cups.

2 cups Alphonso mango juice
3 tbsp granulated sugar
2 tbsp corn flour
4 tsp lemon juice
2 tbsp orange squash
a few drops orange colour

1. Mix the mango juice, sugar, corn flour and 1½ cups of water and boil until the mixture becomes thick.
2. Blend in a liquidiser.
3. Add the lemon juice, orange squash and colour. Use as required.

PEACH SAUCE

✠ Preparation time : 5 minutes. ✠ Cooking time: 5 minutes. ✠ Makes 2 cups.

1 small can (450 gms) peaches
2 level tsp corn flour
2 tsp sugar
2 tsp lemon juice

1. Chop the peaches. Keep aside the syrup.
2. To the fruit syrup, add the corn flour and sugar.
3. Boil for a little time, while stirring continuously, till it becomes thick. Then add the lemon juice and peaches. Use as required.

FRESH MANGO ICE-CREAM

✠ Preparation time : 5 minutes. ✠ No cooking. ✠ Serves 6.

2 tbsp chopped Alphonso mango
pulp of 1 Alphonso mango
200 grams fresh cream
1½ cups full fat milk
¾ cup sugar

1. Set the control of the freezer compartment of the refrigerator at the coolest point one hour in advance.
2. Keep aside a few mango pieces for decoration. Mix the remaining chopped mango, mango pulp and sugar very well.
3. Beat the cream lightly. Add the beaten cream and the milk to the mixture.
4. Pour the mixture into ice trays. The layer of an ice-cream mixture should not be more than 12 mm. (½") thick.
5. Put the trays in the freezer compartment so that each tray touches the chilling plate directly. Under no circumstances should a tray be put over ice cubes or another tray.
6. The ice-cream will be almost fully set in 45 minutes to 1 hour (depending on the

refrigerator).
7. While serving, remove the frozen mixture into a bowl.
8. Mix well, decorate with the remaining mango pieces and serve immediately.

KAJU KOPRA SHEERA

✠ Preparation time : 10 minutes. ✠ Cooking time: 15 minutes. ✠ Serves 4.

1 cup (100 gms) coarsely powdered cashewnuts
1 cup freshly grated coconut
¾ cup sugar
¼ tsp cardamom (elaichi) powder
a few saffron (kesar) strands
4 tbsp ghee

For the garnish
4 to 6 cashewnuts, broken into pieces

1. Heat the ghee in a heavy bottomed pan add sauté the cashewnuts and coconut in it for 7 to 10 minutes over medium heat, stirring continuously. The mixture should be very lightly browned.
2. Add the sugar with ½ cup of water and cook till the sugar dissolves (approx. 5 minutes).
3. Add the cardamom and saffron and mix well.
   Serve warm garnished with the cashewnut pieces.

Basic Recipes

HOW TO COOK PASTA

✠ No preparation. ✠ Cooking time: 10 to 15 minutes. ✠ Makes 2¼ cups.

1½ cups dried pasta (penne, spaghetti, fusilli, conchiglie, fettuccine, macaroni)
1 tbsp oil (for cooking)
1 tbsp oil (for tossing)
1 tsp salt

1. Boil plenty of water in a large pan with 1 tsp of salt and 1 tbsp of oil.
2. Add the pasta to the boiling water by adding little at a time.
3. Cook uncovered, stirring occasionally and gently until the pasta is tender. Cooking times, may vary with the size and the thickness of the pasta. Very small pasta (like macaroni, fusilli, conchiglie, penne) may cook in 5 to 7 minutes.
4. Immediately drain the cooked pasta into a sieve or a colander. Transfer to a bowl of cold water to refresh it. Drain again and keep aside.
5. If the pasta is not to be used immediately, add 1 tbsp of oil to it and toss it.

STEAMED RICE

✠ Preparation time : 5 minutes. ✠ Cooking time: 15 minutes. ✠ Makes 4 cups.

1 cup long grained rice
2 tbsp oil
1 tsp salt

1. Wash the rice thoroughly and soak in 3 cups of water for 30 minutes. Drain and keep aside.
2. Boil 6 to 8 cups of water, add salt and 1 tbsp of oil.
3. Add the rice to the boiling water. Cook till the rice is 85% cooked.
4. Pour into a colander and let the water drain out. Pour some cold water on the rice to arrest further cooking.
5. Let all the water from the rice drain out ensuring that the rice does not contain any moisture.
6. Add the remaining 1 tbsp of oil and toss the rice in it
7. Spread the cooked rice on a flat surface till it is cool.
   Use as required.

BREAD TARTLETS

✠ Preparation time : 2 minutes. ✠ No cooking. ✠ Makes 10 tartlets.
✠ Baking time : 10 minutes. ✠ Baking temperature : 230°C (450°F).

10 slices fresh bread
soft butter for greasing and brushing

1. Remove the crust from the slices.
2. Roll each slice with a rolling pin.
3. Press the rolled slices into the cavities of a muffin tray which is lightly greased with butter.
4. Brush with melted butter and bake in a hot oven at 230°C (450°F) for 8 to 10 minutes or until crisp and serve with a choice of your favourite fillings.